Unbelievable Pictures and Facts About Egypt

By: Olivia Greenwood

Introduction

Egypt is a country that is famous for its pyramids. The ancient Egyptian people were one of the oldest civilizations in the entire world. Today is your opportunity to learn many exciting facts and information about Egypt.

Were any famous movies shot in Egypt?

Over the years a couple of famous movies have been shot in Egypt. These movies include Gods of Egypt, The Mummy, and The Mummy Returns.

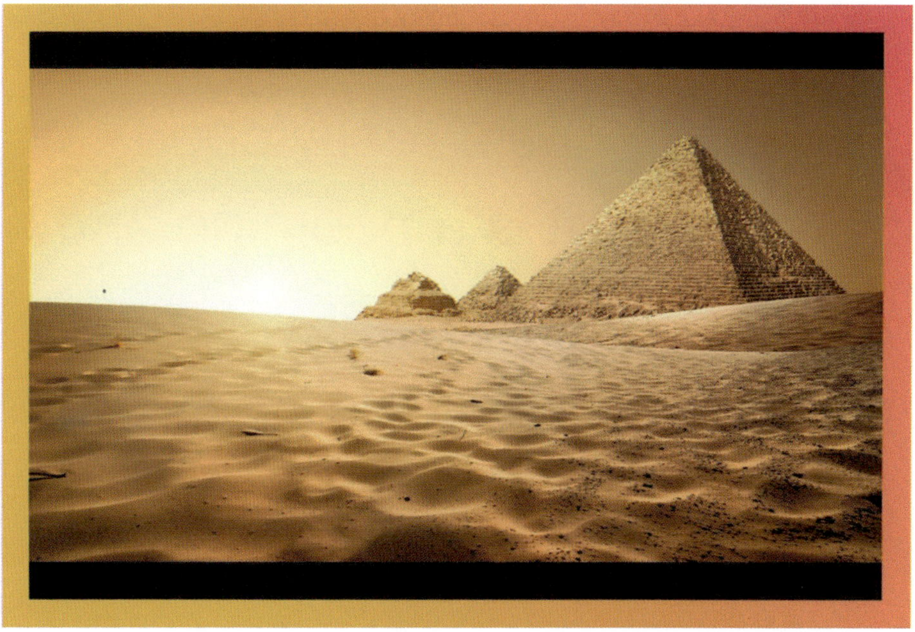

Does Egypt have a very good economy?

Egypt has a really good economy, it is a booming and very successful economy.

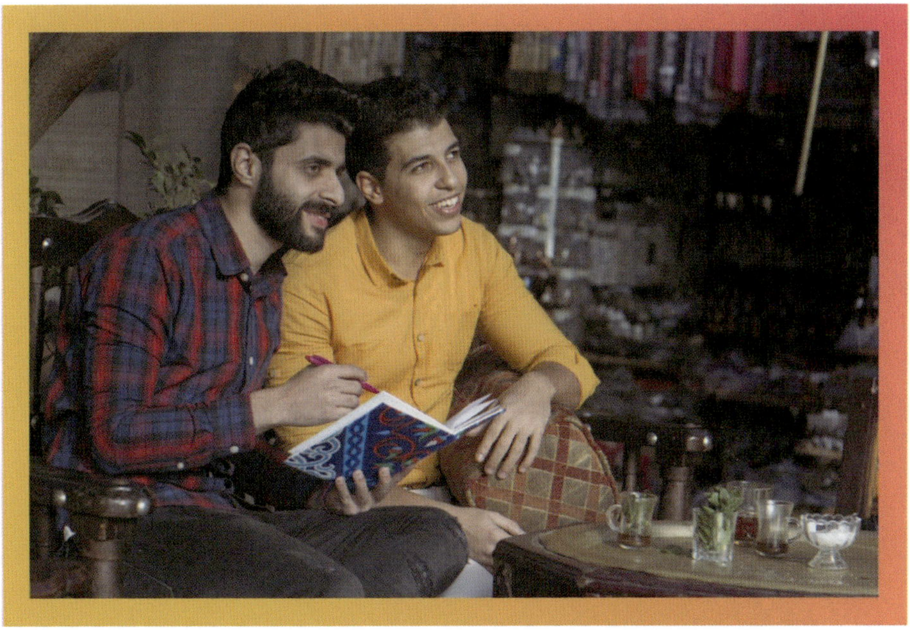

Will you find many museums in Egypt?

Egypt is home to many wonderful and exciting museums. Some of the museums include the Egyptian Museum and the Coptic Museum.

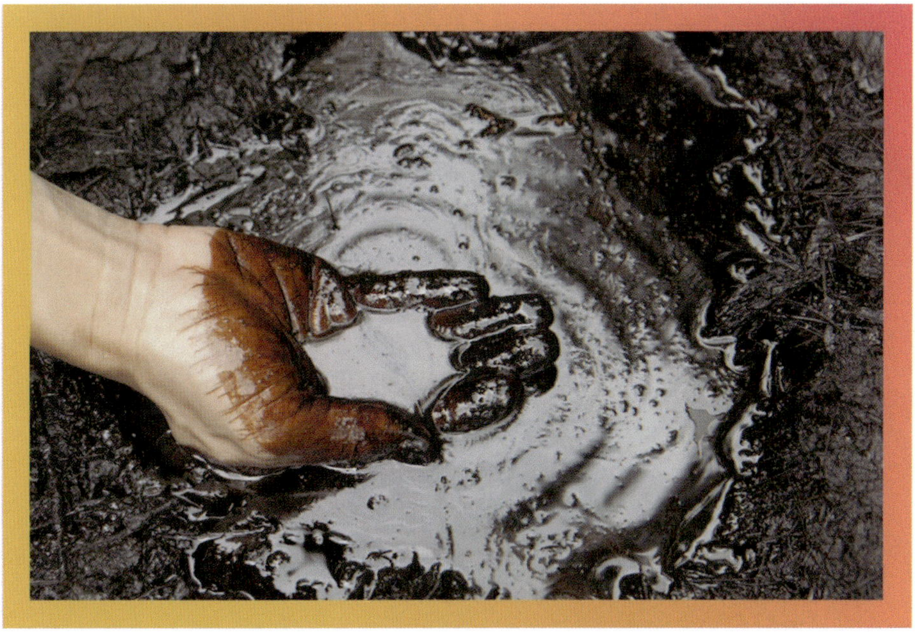

What age do people live up until in Egypt?

The majority of people in Egypt live for around 72 years. Some people even live even longer.

عيد مبارك

Eid Mubarak

Which flower is the national one of Egypt?

The country has its own national flower which is called the Egyptian Lotus.

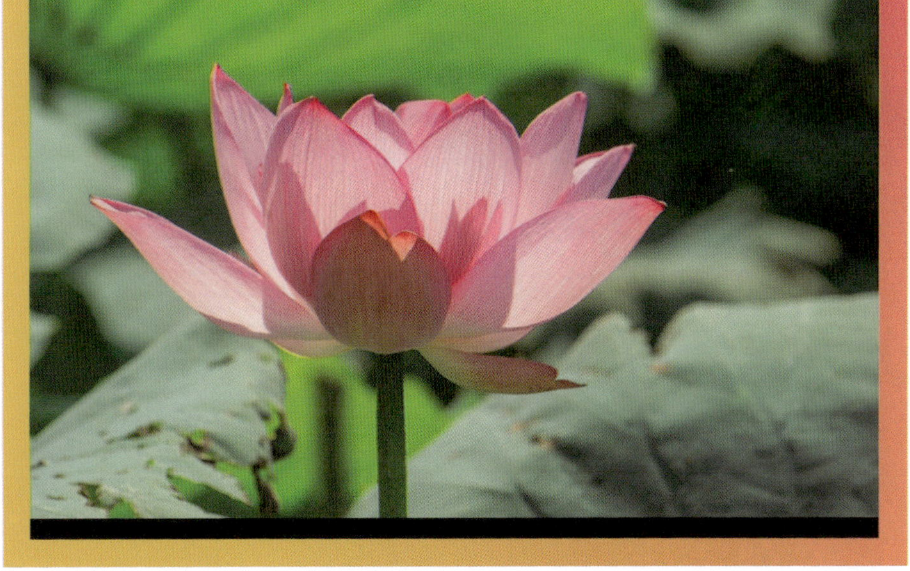

Were the ancient Egyptian people able to write?

People in ancient Egypt wrote in a language called hieroglyphs. This is a very difficult and complicated language with all types of markings and images to it.

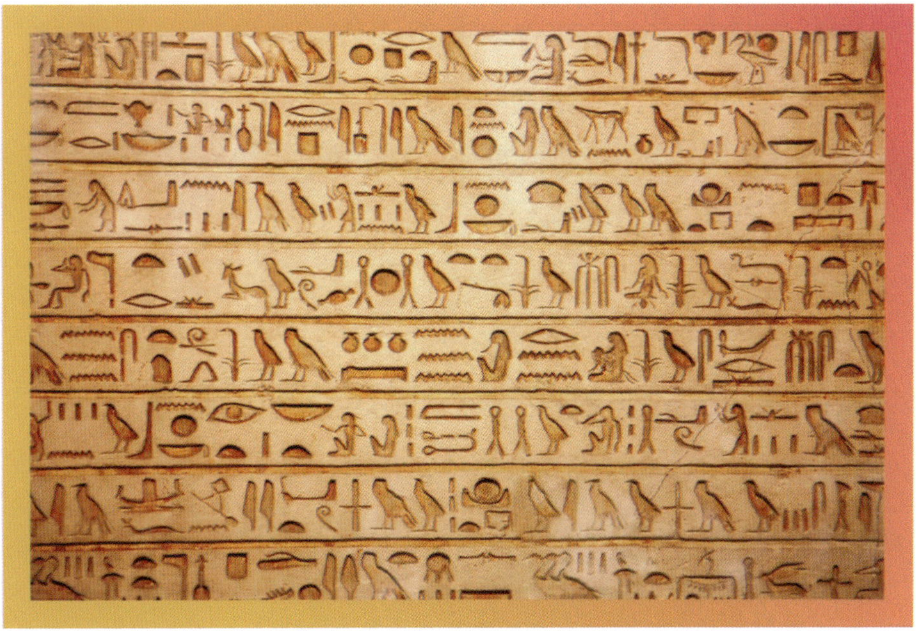

Is Egypt home to any wonders of the world?

Egypt is in fact home to one of the wonders of the world. The Great Pyramid which is situated at Giza attracts millions of tourists from all over the world.

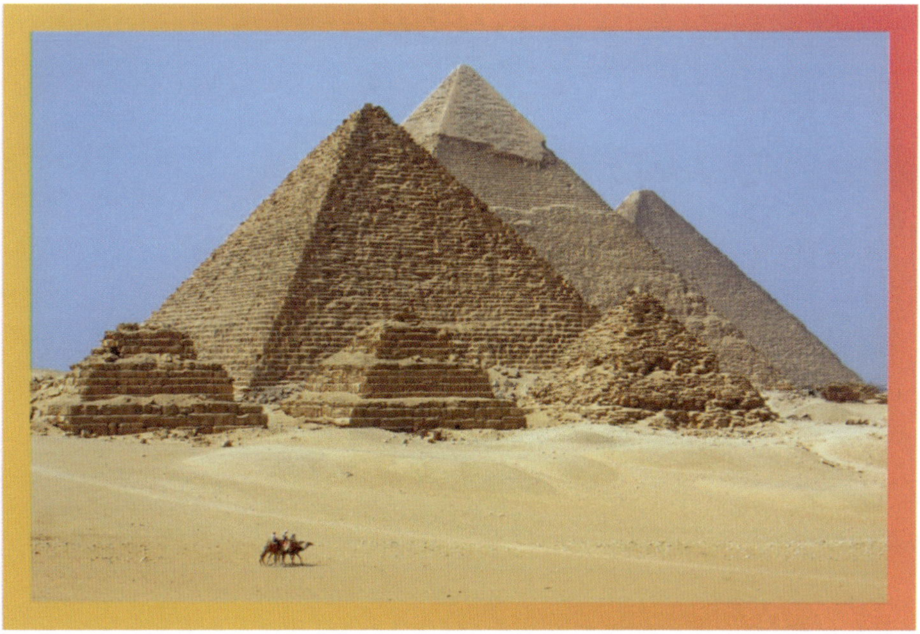

What are some of the main cities in the country?

There are a couple of main cities which includes Giza, Alexandria and the capital Cairo.

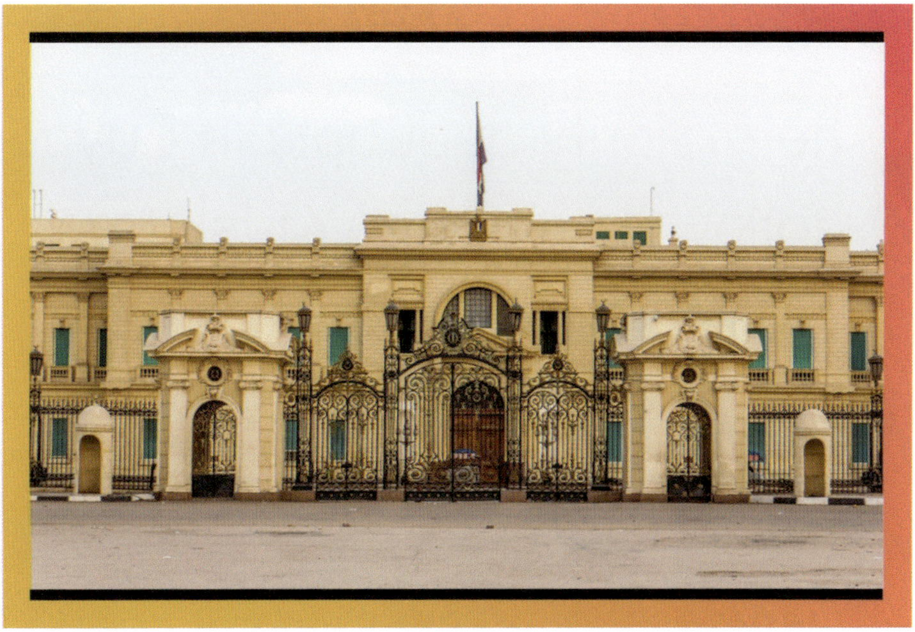

Which religion do people follow in Egypt?

The majority of people in Egypt follow the religion of Islam.

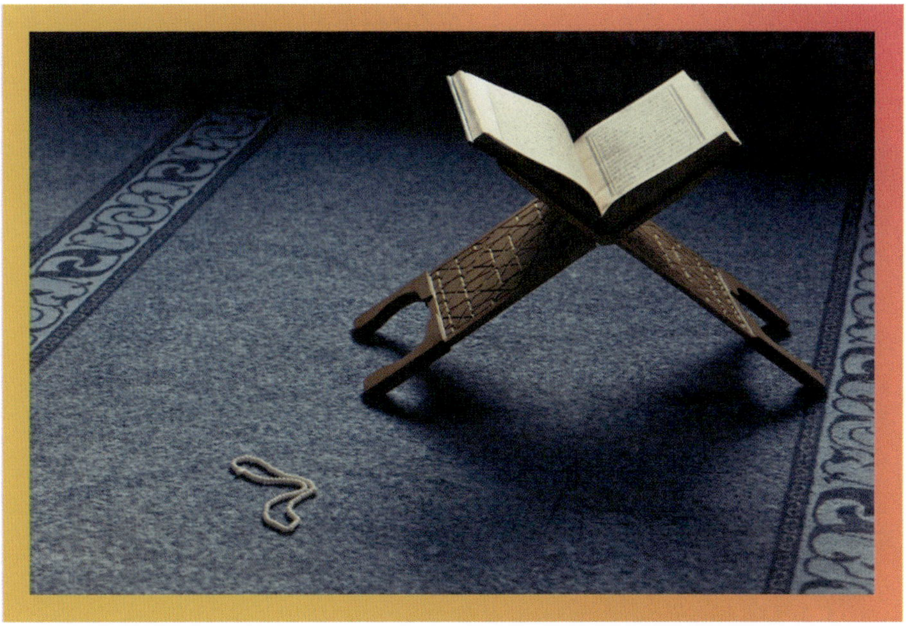

Do many people come to visit the country of Egypt?

Tourism is a big part of Egypt's economy and millions of people come to visit Egypt each and every year, without fail.

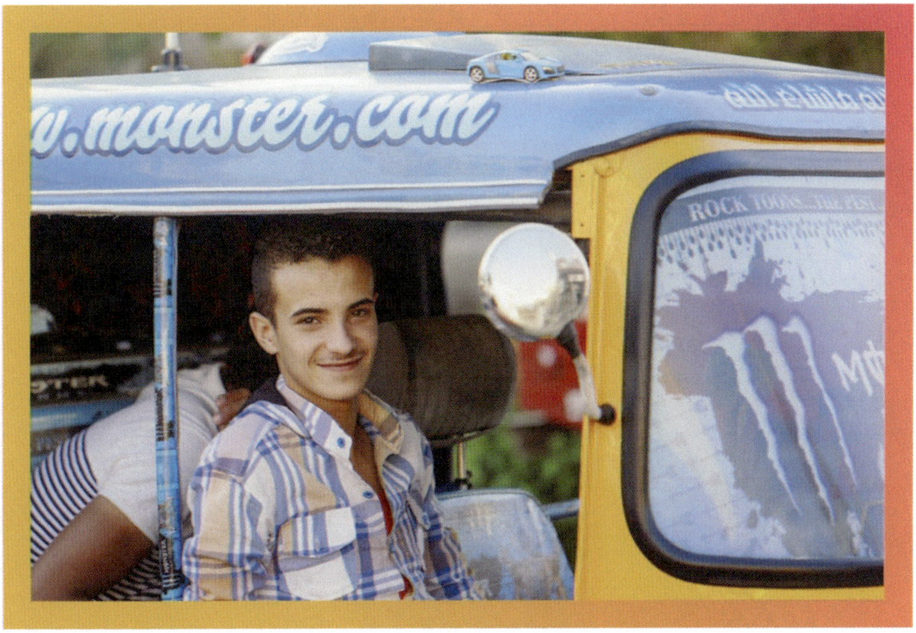
v.monster.com

Is Egypt a big or small country?

Egypt is a very big country and it is known to be one of the bigger countries in the world.

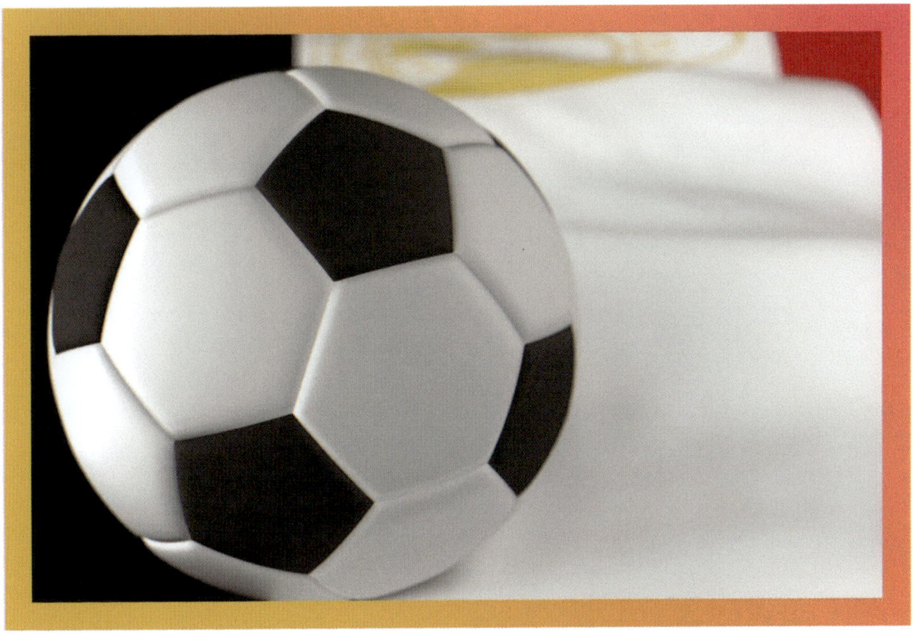

What currency do they use in Egypt?

In order to purchase things in the country of Egypt, you will need to make use of the Egyptian pound.

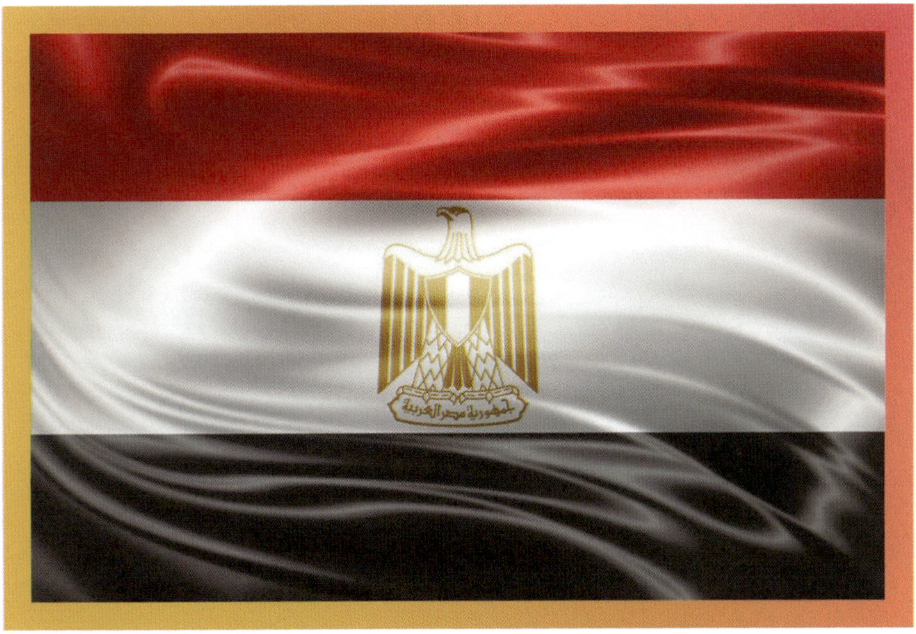
جمهورية مصر العربية

What languages do they speak in Egypt?

You will hear a few different languages being spoken in the country of Egypt. Many people speak French and English but the main language which people speak is Arabic.

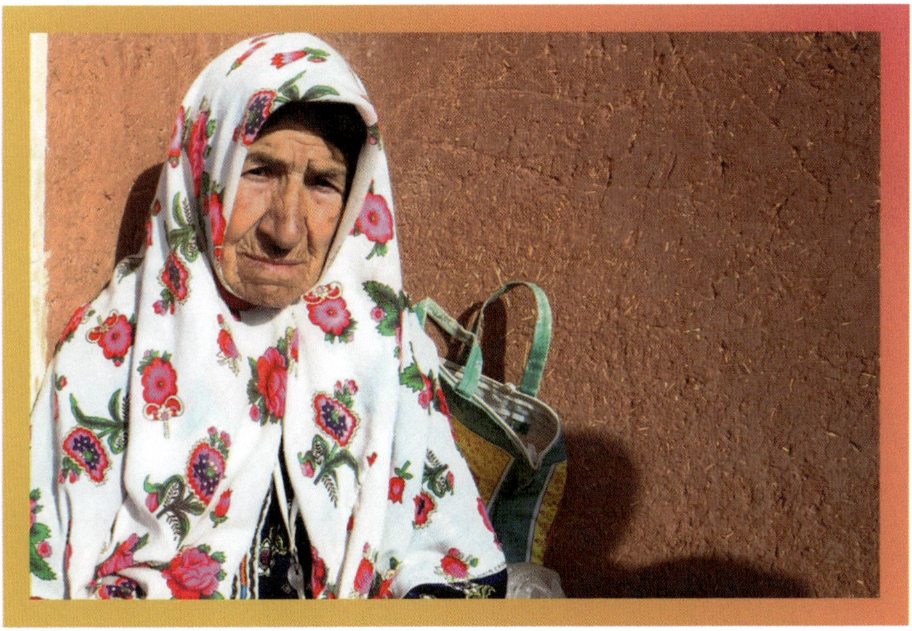

Will you discover any animals in Egypt?

Do you know anything about camels? They are very interesting animals and they are famous for living in Egypt. You will also find many other unique animals such as the sand cat and the sand rat.

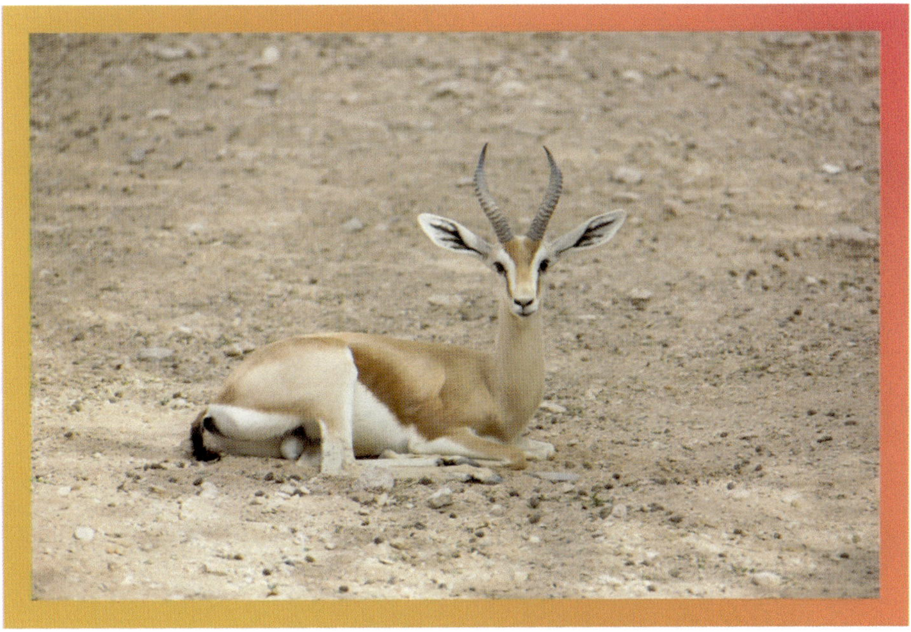

Which river is the longest in Egypt?

Have you ever heard of a river called the Nile river? This is the longest river in the country and it plays a very significant part in people's lives. It is a major contributor towards the water, transportation and much more.

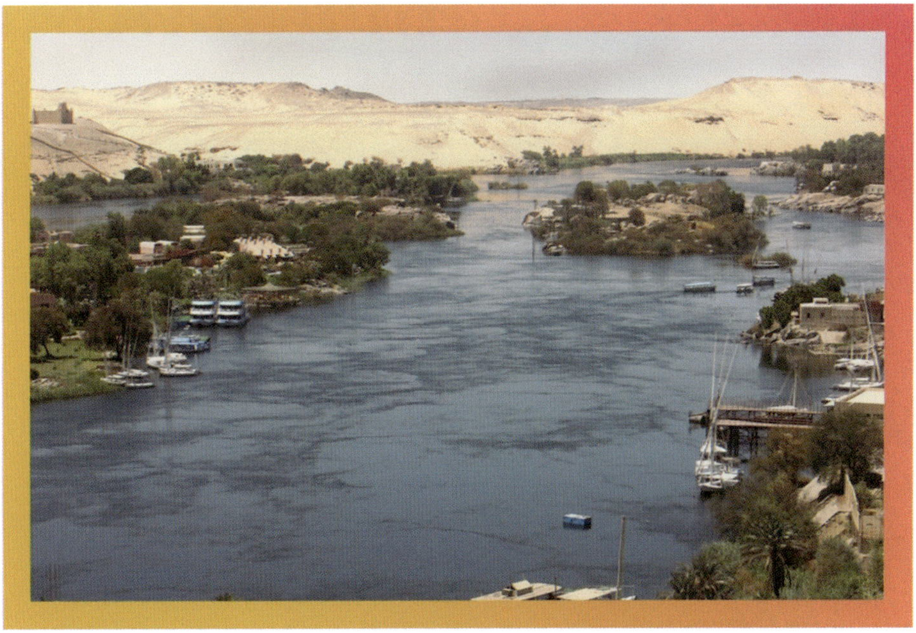

What type of weather does Egypt have?

People know the country of Egypt for being extremely hot and dry. The reason why the climate is so dry is because of all the desert land in the country. During summer the weather can reach very high temperatures.

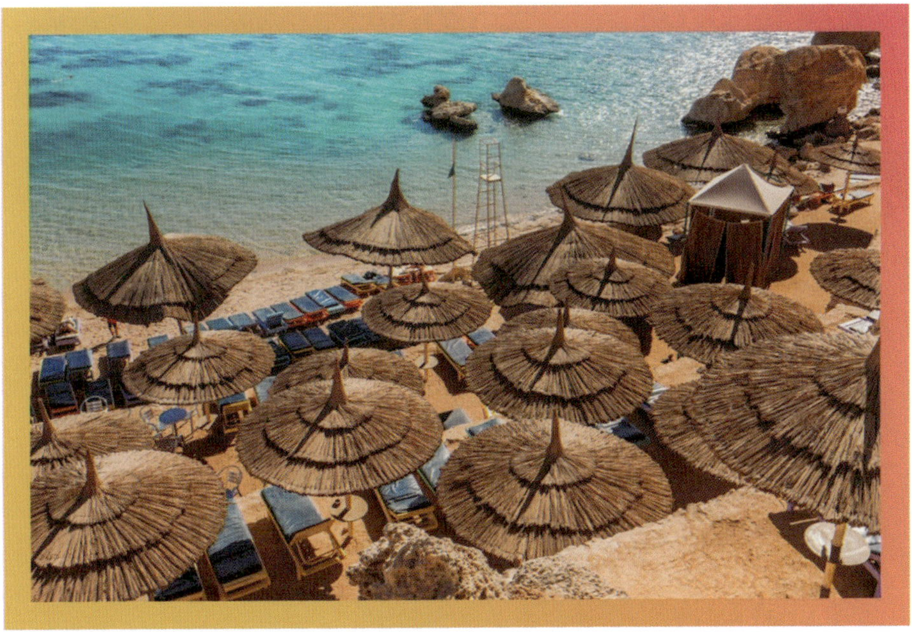

What is the population amount in Egypt?

Many people live in the country of Egypt. There are currently over 97.58 million people living in the country.

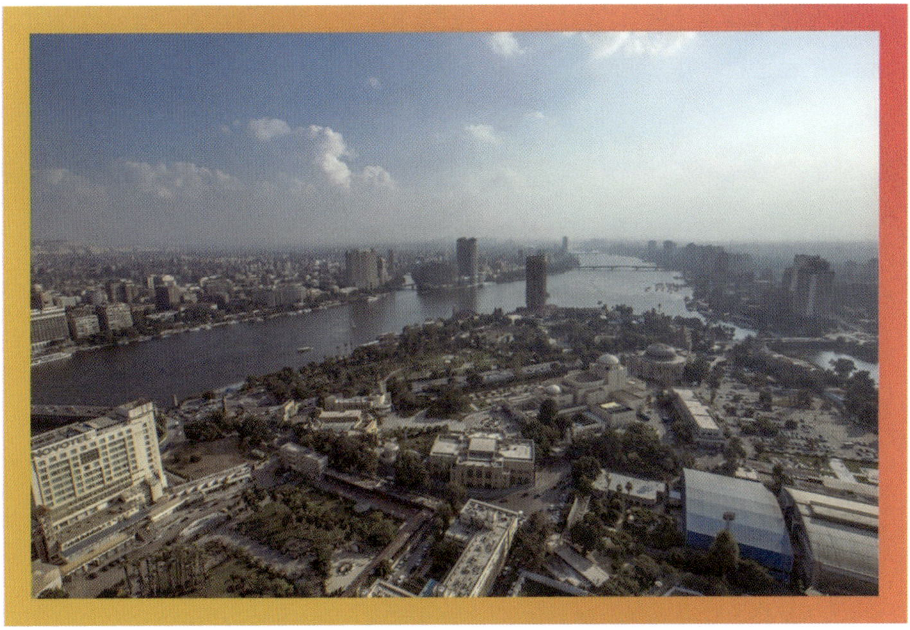

What type of landscape does the country have?

The country is well-known for having a huge desert. It is also home to the long Nile river and many mountains.

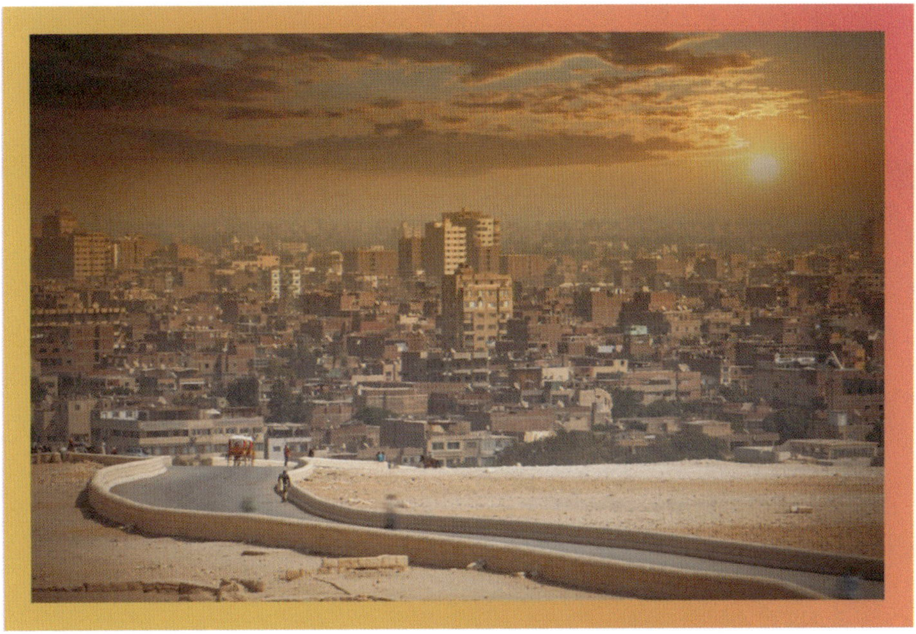

Where in the world will you locate Egypt?

Do you know how to find the African continent on the map? Try looking for Northern Africa and you should find Egypt. If you are still struggling try looking for Sudan, Libya or Israel and you will soon spot Egypt.

ZYPERN
Nikosia
Larnaka
Lemesos
Tartus
Trablous
LIBANON
BEIRUT
DAMASKUS
Homs
1803
3107
Haifa
Nazareth
Mafraq
ISRAEL
Tel Aviv
Jericho
AMMAN
Jerusalem
Port Said
Gaza
El Arîsh
JORDANIEN
ALEXANDRIA
Tanta
El-Alamein
Shibîn el-Kom
GIZEH
KAIRO
Suez
Suezkanal
Sinai
Ma'an
Elat
El Aqaba
PYRAMIDEN
Medinet el-Faijûm
KATHARINEN-KLOSTER
Za'farâna
Beni Suêf
Baharija-Oasen
El Bawiti
Beni Mazâr
Mt. Sinai
2285
2403
Tabuk
El Minia
Mallawî
Golf von Suez
G. von Aqaba
Sharm-el-Sheikh
Râs Muhammad
Harrat al 'Uwayrid
Duba
Dairût
Assiut

Which city in Egypt is the capital one?

The capital city is also the biggest city in the country. This city goes by the name of Cairo.

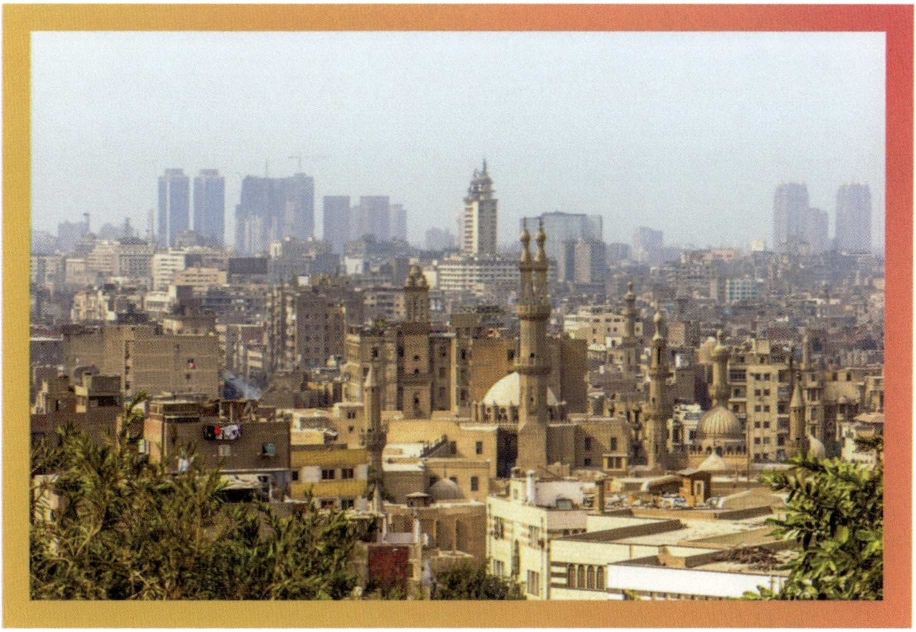

Printed in Great Britain
by Amazon